Thoughts in a Journal

LAURA ZARCONI

Copyright © 2021 Laura Zarconi
All rights reserved
First Edition

PAGE PUBLISHING, INC.
Conneaut Lake, PA

First originally published by Page Publishing 2021

ISBN 978-1-6624-2637-7 (pbk)
ISBN 978-1-6624-2638-4 (digital)

Printed in the United States of America

This book never would have been possible without the support of my family. I have to thank my family: my mom and my dad for never giving up on me, my brother and sister for giving me things to write about, my son for being a muse to me, and for those people that always told me that I'd never make it. I have to thank you too. You lit a fire under me to keep writing. Most of all, I have to thank everyone for their never-ending support. Without you, none of this would be possible. Thank you, and this book is for you.

Contents

The Special One 9
River's Tale 11
Darken Forest 13
Pleading Eyes 14
Darkness All Around 15
Unfair Life 16
Rain-Filled Nights 17
Age-Old Question 18
Abuse Me 19
Unforgotten 21
Loved Ones 22
Cruel World 23
Every Word a Lie 24
Eventually 25
Abandoned 26
Used 28
Liar 29
Inside the Box 30
Evil 31
Words Inside a Journal 32
Mad from the Morning Light 34
Letter to My Son 35
Through the Rain 38
Breathing Easier 39
Borrowed Angel 40
Here with Me Now 41
In the Rain 42

With These Tears	43
Looking Glass	44
Inside the Tornado	46
Drowning	47
Silver Blade	48
Guilt	50
So Long I	52
Remembering How to Live	53
Decade	54
Thank You	55
How Is It Possible	56
Grandfathers	57
Hunter's Birthday Letter	59
A Thank-You to a Soldier	61
Reflections	62
Hollow Heart	63
Blind Eye	64
Dream Come True	66
Are You with Me?	67
The Hawk and the Phoenix	68
End Times	69
Misunderstood	70
Crimson Regret	71
Untold Secret	73
Locked Inside	74
Long Lost Words	75
Eraser	76
In Your Arms	77
Lost	78
Once Again	80
In a Glass Globe	81
Nightmare	82

As You Slumber 83
Angel of Death 84
My Brian 85
Voids 87
Fool Again 88
Waiting for Me 89
Living Hell 90
You Found Me 91
Souls United 92
Never Understood 93
Hold on to You 95
Friday Night 96
Simply You 98
The Fall We Fear 99

The Special One

I stand upon a shore forgotten and watch the waves at my feet.

Knowing in my soul that no one would believe the tales that I have to tell.

It would seem that without even knowing my soul has been blessed. Now I try so hard to remember what it was like to feel so alone.

I try to remember the day I lost the pain and saw the glory of life again.

Slowly my mind wanders to a time so long ago forgotten. I know that in my mind's eye that I was a blind fool for so long. I thought that I was okay and that I needed no one but myself.

For some reason while I stand upon this Scotland shore, I think of you.

Knowing that the almighty put you in my life for reasons no mortal could ever understand. For the longest time, I run and hide from my feeling. I never wanted that wall to fall and then you walked in the door. It seemed that the fates were against me then, my eyes were opened to a world I never knew existed.

Without you knowing you were given a gift. So many lives you have touched, and so many hearts you have warmed. You say you know not why you are so special. But to look at you is to look upon an angel's face. Your voice rings sweeter than a Sunday choir. The stars are nothing in comparison to you. I will forever hold this last memory of you deep within my soul.

As the waves crash on the rocks below me, I think of you. Always hearing that gifted voice in my heart. Knowing that when all seems lost, the stars will forever guide my path, you, a friend so far away yet not long forgotten. Remember these few words that I give to you. Nothing last forever, yet it seems if we try hard enough, we can reach ever after.

Feeling a mist so long missed as I stand here and watch the stars. Knowing that one of them you could be wishing on. If I close my eyes, I can still see your smile and know that for all the sad times in our lives, we meet that special one and will never be without them. Though there are miles between us, I feel like I have never been closer to you.

Wake up on a Sunday morning and know that the church bells will soon be ringing. The birds are flying through this clear and peaceful morning air. Today will be that day when you will find that peace you have longed for. Shall I be there for it? Nay. Not in body but in sprit I shall forever be with you.

If one morning I should not awake, I know that I will not be forgotten. Nothing shall be left unsaid, for you know my deepest fears. I only ask this one thing. Please remember me.

River's Tale

This river has a tale to tell. Shall you stay to hear it? You asked me once if I was scared. How can I not be with the tale you are about to hear? For once long ago, a young maiden born to a lord and lady was sitting upon this very bank. Tear that filled this once dry bank were shed for the loss of the one she loved. Still young and still so innocent. Her maiden eyes beheld a sight that was once only a fairy tale told to her as a babe.

Out of the shadow arose a unicorn. So black and mighty. His body gleamed in the moonlight. The maiden watched as he tossed his magnificent head and raised on his hind legs. His cry echoing through the woods but falling only upon her ears. "Come thy love. Be my wife in a land not so far away." The maiden stood frozen in fear for it was the voice of her beloved. Slowly she walked to the mighty beast and reached out a hand. His silver hair soft to her touch. His eyes had fire dancing in their depths. "My love 'tis it really you?" She whispered. "Yes, my love. Come and be my queen." The wind whispered.

Far away a land unknown, there is a river that on the bank when the moon is full you can hear the cry of the mighty unicorn. The river, the only one that is filled with salted water. Its gentle soothing sound is of a whispered cry. Some say if you stand on the shores and your heart is pure, the deepest desire you wish for will be granted. When these few words are spoken. "Come, my love. So we can be. As we should have been from thus day one. Although you seem forgotten, my love for you still burns. I call thee to come rescue me. On the winds of time. On this river of tears. I call thee to be with me forever more."

Take this warning and listen to these words. Only the purest of love can bring a magic like that. So when the world seems to be against you and the love you crave so far away. Come to the River of Tears and taste your life again.

Darken Forest

Standing here in this dark and forgotten forest. Trying hard to remember what brought me to this point. Watching the blackened water of this endless pool call my name. All this time, I thought that I could live in your world. How was I to know that it was all a lie, and it was just a cruel, inhumane joke? All these times, you told me I was something; I was nothing. All the words you told me were a lie. Never wanted it to end this way. Didn't want to be alone in this world, but it seems I am destined to remain forever forgotten. Don't know why I dreamed the dreams I did. All I wanted was not for me. Time and time again, others tried to warn me not to live the fool's dream.

Now I sit here trying to find the pieces of my life that seemed to have become forgotten to you. All I was to you was an easy catch. Never really cared. The games you played have left me mad. Staring at this pool trying to piece it all together. Tell me now why you did what you did to me. Why was I the one you picked for this? Did I really make it that easy for you? Was I that naïve? Didn't you care at all? Tell me now what I want to know!

I hate that I made it so easy for you. All I saw was warm arms that wanted to hold me tight when I needed to be held. I hate you for treating me as you did. I was never important to you. You killed me from the inside out. Slowly I let you take his place. Never again did I think I would be with someone who treated me as he did. I was worthless in his eyes. Just a trophy to hang on the wall. Your lies feel like his fists. The rage I feel inside can never compare to the hatred I see when I look in my eyes. You turned me into something that I hate. A weak little nothing that will once again stand alone!

Pleading Eyes

I look at you and see the ghost of what we once had. Never thought it would come to this. For so long, I hid these marks. Tears of rage now fill my eyes. Hatred I never knew now fills my world. All those long nights you would tell me I was special; I was really nothing to you. Just a target for you to practice on.

Now I stand here with a smoky look in my eyes and an empty soul. I am a hollow shell of who I once was. I have lost the will to live because I know I have nothing more to give. I just want to be set free of these dreadful memories. Every time I close my eyes, I see your fist flying toward me.

Looking in this mirror, I do not know whom this person is staring back at me. I see a pleading look in her eyes that are so filled with sadness. As I back away, I realize I am staring at what I have become. Never thought that I would become something I would not be able to look at.

So long ago, I thought myself strong. I never would have let it come to this if I was as strong as I thought I was. Voices swim in my head telling me to end the pain. That there will be no end to the torment I am in.

Laying in a field finally having come to a rest. No sound can touch me. My eyes no longer see. I feel no pain. As I watch, I see the ones who left me to my pain mourn their loss. Forever gone are the pleading looks.

Darkness All Around

Raging storm clouds roll across the sky. Lighting flashes in her eyes. She knows that she has been taken for a fool. Never again will that ever happen. Slowly she runs from the house before the noise can be heard. The bells in the village cover her cries. Never did she think it would come to this.

Standing in a wooded place staring at herself feeling shame for the loss of control she had tonight. Never again will that ever happen. Lighting overhead flashes, but she seems not to notice. All she hears is the voice that seems to control her. She is his puppet. He needs only pull the strings, and she shall dance.

So, it has come to this. Nothing else can ever be the same again. For he has pulled his last string. As they lower his body into the cold dank ground, she watches. Her mind is numb, her body tells her she will miss his dreadful touch. His lying word and his cruel words. Laughter bubbles in her chest and can barely be contained.

People come and tell her how lucky she was to have been gone the night that their lord was laid to rest. No one sees the flashing in her eyes that tells them how blind they have been. He had taken more from her than her body. He had taken her light.

Unfair Life

As a child, you have no choice but to live by the rule that you are handed. Your voice is one that no one listens to, it is an unfamiliar sound. Adults never listen. They look on you as though you are a program that never needs to be nurtured.

Time reveals that there is not much change when you are grown. You were raised to fit the impossible standard. Never knowing what will be asked of you next. Always questioning what will be taken from you until you are a nervous ball of nothingness. No one willing to tell you what shadow you will be asked to fill next.

Can't they see what they are doing to you? Is it that hard for them to see that you are still, in many ways, that quivering child sitting in the corner trying to tell your family that just because you are young does not mean you are wrong?

Is it so much to ask to be treated as a human and not just something that is in the way of their living? Never wanting to cause any trouble you do you feel is the right thing to do. Always feeling as though you are backed against the wall. Fighting a fight that you know will never be won.

Is it fair that a child should be programmed, and if they choose to do something that is not in the setup of their life that they are cast aside and forgotten, never to be asked about again? Should anyone have to live up to this standard?

Rain-Filled Nights

Can you see the clouds from where you are? Is it so far away that you can't see the mist beginning to fall? Have you forgotten what we once had together? Do you call out to me in the heat of the summer nights only to be answered by the dark? When you close your eyes, is it my face you see?

You were my one true love. No one will compare to you. I never want to feel the pain I did when you walked out of my life. Every night, I lay awake thinking of what you meant to me. I hear your voice calling me on the darkest nights. Regret for not telling you all you meant to me fills my soul. Never should have asked you to leave. Now I wish I could hold you again.

When the clouds part, are you smiling down at me? Can you see me from where you sit? Did I truly mean as much to you as you said I did? Can't you tell them they made a mistake? It's not your time to be there. That you need to be with the one that you love? Can you come back and hold me?

It's been raining in my heart since you walked out that door. Still see your smile as you tell me you will see me soon. I can still feel your arms holding me while we watch the rain slid down the window. It's your lips I feel caressing my skin tonight. Can you come to me? Is it truly over? Tell me I am dreaming and this pain is not real. Tell me that you are still here and you still love me so.

Age-Old Question

Do you ever sit in the rain and wonder why it rains? Have you ever looked at a child and wondered why they are so carefree? When you see couples walking in the park, do you often think what it was like for them before they met? When you see two very close friends, does it cross your mind that they might not truly be friends?

I have sat here and wondered why so many are brought into my life only to leave me hurt again? Why is it this one hurts more than any other? Why do I care so much? Why is it so easy for you to walk out on this friendship and not shed a tear? Am I the only one who sees that we were meant to be friends?

Can you feel my pain? Do you see the pain in my eyes as I look at you? Are you blind to my tears? My heart is ripping, and you can't seem to help. I am not picking up the pieces this time. I will leave them as they lay. In the wind blowing like the dust we bury the dead in. For without you, I am dead.

Abuse Me

I'm the child who sits in the corner listening to their parents fight. I'm the one who keeps their pain locked up and out of sight. I am the outcast at school who has no friends. I'm the child who cries each night.

I'm the one everyone wishes would kill themselves. I'm the one whose life is torn. I'm the one who watches the cliques go by. They point and laugh out loud. I'm the one in school with the eating disorder who will never be in the "in" crowd. I'm the teen who turns to drugs and darkness and gets lost in depression's cloud.

Abuse me. You know you want to.

Abuse me, I'm an easy target.

I'm the adult who can't speak their mind. I'm the one you looked right through. I'm the person sitting in the corner crying. I'm the one you target your anger to. I'm the one who can't stand up for themselves. I'm the one screaming for your abuse. Never going to defend myself, I'm not even going to move.

I'm the one who held on to the hope that you'd love me. I'm the one you killed inside. I was the release of your anger; it was me you called me nothing. I screamed to be abused with pride.

The child with the parents is now looking through bars.

The teen in school wears the scars of the blade.

The outcast at school is in the news every day.

The adult is standing six feet tall from six feet in the ground. Forever remembered for their one last stand. Now they're feeling proud.

I'm the one you abused.

Look at me now.

Unforgotten

I feel your arms wrapped around my heart. I still feel your
Lips caressing my skin. When I close my eyes, I see you smiling at me.
I hear your voice in the rain whispering softly. Three words I long to
Hear again. I love you. Tears stream down my cheeks. My heart beats
Its soft sad beat.
Slowly as the days turn to months, I start to feel you fade.
There's no comfort in the night. No longer do I hear your voice.
All alone I stand. Cold, icy rain wraps itself tightly around
My now shattered heart.

So alone in my heart. Now I start to take those steps.
Slowly I piece my heart back together. I can say
Your name and smile with the memories that I
Hold tightly in my mind.

That day will never come when I forget you. You'll
Always hold that one place that no one can take
From you. Even in death, you're still my heart's desire.

Loved Ones

Sitting in a world filled with hate, asking myself every day what the point behind living is. Watched the news again tonight just to hear another story of terror is being covered. People killing people. Students carrying guns to school. Not even safe in churches. Trying hard to find a peaceful place where I can come to rest. This is the world we live in. Where our children play in unsafe places. Never knowing when the next unfaithful event will take place.

Every night when you kiss your loved ones good night, you pray for one last moment to tell them how you really feel. When you watch your best friend drive away after a day of fun, you pray they know how deeply you care for them.

In this place we live in, you never have tomorrow promised. It can all be taken away in the snap of a finger. Never go to bed angry. Never leave your friends or family on hateful words. Nothing is promised.

Cruel World

So many people think they know the answers. There is more than one way to end dispute. Why does it have to end with babies behind bars? Where were the parents? Can anyone answer that?

So many kids killing kids over nothing. A simple misunderstanding turns to guns and knives. Can't people see they're killing our future? Are they truly blind to the fate we have in store if this act continues?

When times get tough, can't we turn to each other in love and not war? Is it too late to change the world's cruel fate? Where were the parents at when their baby was gunned down? When somebody's little girl was selling herself to feed her baby. Where were they when another as a young child lays in their own blood. Can't people see it's time for a change?

Every Word a Lie

You live your life as a child looking to adults for all the answers. Sometimes, the ones you receive are pretty normal, but others just seem to be too bizarre to even think of. As the weeks change to years, you start the learning by mistakes. Your parents sit back and watch you with a disappointing stare. Nothing pleases them. You are not that child who used to question everything.

Every word of love was nothing but a lie. No one in the house really cares if you are there or gone. Only when it suits the purpose do they start to wonder where you could be.

Growing up around a world of anger. Blackness takes your heart in its cold cruel hands and laughs as you cry for salvation. You walk this earth seeing nothing but lies in every word you hear. What has taken away your innocence, is it that you were treated so coldly? Was it you felt that your family has abandoned you as you asked your questions? Does it make you think that you are the cause?

Are you a soul branded by ambition? Does that cast you as the disappointment in the family? Do you care?

Eventually

Sitting in the center of the crazy life. Watching the pain flare in other's eyes. Seeing that the pain and numbness is all around in full effect. I sit back and laugh at your discomfort. I see you clawing the earth as it falls around your cold body. No one cares that you are still here. They would, just as soon see you suffer as they are. Nothing in their eyes is warm. They smile and laugh as you walk past them. Haven't you noticed that nothing you do is going to cause you to fit into their world? You could never be good enough.

Join me in this life I live. Nothing touches. No pain is felt. All you see is what your heart knows is true. No one in the place you are is there to be a hand. They stand by and wait. They know you will not be there forever. They will rejoice the day you leave this earth.

Standing in the center of a busy highway of people. What caused you to pull the trigger? What did he do to hurt you so? Was it that he rejected you? Did he hurt you when he stole your innocence? Was it that he abused you when you asked to be abused? Was that the final step to this destruction?

Your family left you in my hands. I am the one you cry to at night. I am the pain you feel every day. I am the blackness you slip into as the drugs flow through your veins. Have you not noticed that there is someone holding your hand when no other wishes to touch your blackened soul? I am the soft whisper that you hear in your head. Let yourself feel me inside your body. Let me speak your words. Give yourself to me. I can be your salvation. I can take away the bitterness. I can replace it with the power to overcome all others. Place yourself in my realm, I am the voice of reason when there is no other. I am forever with you. Just call my name. For I am darkness.

Abandoned

Looking back over the years of my life, I see that it was meant to be.

Never really knowing what to do next. Always looking for what was the hidden reason. Never listening to what someone had to say. Kept my heart in a glass box. Wasn't dumb enough to lay it on the line for anyone. Cold and distant was something I mastered as a child. No one could get inside.

Left standing with my heart in shreds. Never really thought it was very wise to let someone in. Now look at the ending to this story. Tears that seem to keep spilling down my pale and hollow face. Looking in your eyes, I see that it never really mattered to you. Everything was a joke to you. Never meant a damn thing to you. All I was is a step for you to reach something that is so out of reach.

Life had no meaning to you until the day you met me. That is what you always told me. How was I to fight a hidden darkness that I never saw coming.

Look at me now. You have been forgotten. Does it bother you that I moved on so soon and that it proves that it was all a lie? Never meant the words I told you. Now it's you, sitting on the dust, picking up the pieces of your broken heart.

I laugh as I watch you make a fool of yourself. Time and time again, you sit there and tell me that I was so important to you. The only thing I was to you was nothing. Well, I am something. Something you can never have again. Something you will never be. There will come a day when you will see me, and I will be beyond your reach. When that day comes, you will see what you walked out on. You will see what pain feels like.

So, until that day…think well.

Used

You used and abused me. Your words have killed me
They still haunt my every being. I let
You in my life and you stole my securities.
I was a lost little girl and you used that to your advantage. Now I'm hollow
Inside. Nothing left to give. An old discarded toy that you grew tired of.
Did it make you happy to see the pain you put me through? Does
It please you to know you've ruined me for anyone else? I
Still hear your words in my head. So hateful and cruel.
Do my cries haunt your twisted mind? Can you still
See the hatred flashing in my eyes? Can't you just leave me alone?
Haven't you hurt me enough? Nothing I do can shake your ghost. It
Haunts my every dream. Dreams of being happy come crashing
Down. You've killed me. Turned me into what I hate.
I live in fear. I cannot love anyone. I have
Become weak. Are you happy now? The tears you've caused
Have burned themselves inside my soul. I never cried
Until I saw what I've become with your help.
This is your work. You kill my soul and turned me weak. You've ruined
My life with your lies. Are you happy now? Every day I try to
Move past. I have a past of being strong and never letting anyone
In. Do you like what you see? It's your hurtful words that ring my
head. This is all because of you.

Liar

I sit and hear your cruel words. You claimed to love me.

Everything you ever told me was a lie. Nothing you said held truth. The lies you told have destroyed me. I was a happy person. Now I see what I missed. I lost my teen years to you. I grew to think everything you said was true. I was worthless.

Less than nothing. No one could love a worthless piece of trash. My head was so fucked because of you. My soul destroyed by your words. I was so much better than you. You were lucky to know me. I was cursed to meet you. I was so strong and full of life. Now I am a weak, worthless person. You are a liar. There was no love from you. Your words hurt worse than your fists.

Rage consumed me. I only see anger.
I walk the road of life alone.
No one tries to come close.
They see what you have done to me.
They all sat by and watched the life drain from my eyes.
Why do I feel this hatred for you?
Could it be the fact that you tore me down so bad you made me hate myself?
It was you that made me feel inadequate.
It was your words that turned me into a coward. You are a liar. I wish you just disappear. The day will come that you will pay for what you did. All the hitting and shoving. All the trash you called me. Every day has its dawn. Too bad yours will never come. You are lower than a liar. You are nonexistent. For that I am grateful.

Inside the Box

Inside the darkened box, one stands staring at the crimson on her hands.

Screams only heard inside her head. Eyes lowered as she walks.

Never worthy of their attention. The tear in the wall slowly growing allowing in the light.

Evils grasp held firmly on her heart. Tears of sorrow go unnoticed.

No one sees the pain she buries deep inside. Slowly crumbling.

Pebble by pebble, her belief in anything good and real slowly faded.

Sitting in a hollow head, only her thoughts consume her. The outside world doesn't see the empty gleam in her eyes. The dust that falls in place of tears.

Ripping, striping, pealing. Section by crimson sections, she peals her skin. Layer by layer, she shows her pain. No eyes will look upon her hideous form. Laughing and ringing inside her empty soul. Day by day, the hand of evil tightens.

Standing on the edge, wondering how it came to this. Pain fills every emotion she feels. Emotions swirl stronger than a tornado in her soul. Eyes empty and glazed. It's too late to change her fate. Air rushes against her face. Falling free. Nothing to stop her decent to the bottom. Ground smiling at the feel of flesh upon its surface.

The voice is silent as she leaves her darkened box. Standing back in the early crimson-skied morning. Her eyes take in the only sight her blind eyes can see. The reflection in the mirror mocking her. The face of a stranger stares back. Placing a hand on the face in her reflection she is greeted with smooth flawlessness. Forever free in her own pain-filled subconscious.

Evil

The steady sound of agony grips our hearts. Forever violence greets us at our door.

Ask ourselves how it came to this. Poisonous gas filling our lungs and the lungs of the unborn. Our hands covered in our brother's blood. Hatred is the only emotion we feel. Love has been abandoned. Anger fills our words with every breath we take. Lust has taken over our minds. Greed consuming us in our fight to reach the top. Shadows fill our mind with every lie we tell. Never hearing the truth is anything. If we heard the truth, could we find it in the mess we've created.

Mothers killing babies. Fathers beating their wives. Evil has come to our door. Will you be the next to allow it in your house? Words spoken in anger brought back with a fist. Blood pouring from your face while you tell them it was an accident. You know he's sorry. You know Mommy didn't mean to hold you under so long. They didn't feel the pain you did. The burning and the panic as you couldn't draw your next breath. The tears you've cried are no more real to them, they once were. Do you still love her every time she hits you? Does his love show every time he plunges his knife inside your still-beating heart?

Babies dying to protect a world that has no reason, can't you feel it? It is breathing on your neck. Do you feel it closing in around your heart? The hatred. The anger. Life no longer matters. Karma goes as karma's given. Does that mean nothing to you? When you look at the sky, do you see the stars or just the vast emptiness? Taste the bloodlust rushing through your veins. Feel the hatred as if it was simply standing beside you. Will you be the one to answer the evil's call?

Words Inside a Journal

Confusion.
Anger.
Lust.
Hatred.
Pain.
Love.
Abandonment.
Hollow.
Void.
Unfilled.
Vacant.
Unsound.
Vacuous.
Empty.
Sunken.
Depressed.
Indented.
Carved out.
Stupid.
Worthless.
Fool.
Dreary.
Lonesome.
Solitary.
Desolate.
Remote.
Sequestered.
Forlorn.
Lone.
Chilly.
Icy.
Dead.

Frigid.
Still.
Extinguished.
Frosty.
Lifeless.
Weak.
Spiritless.
Uninspired.
Unaffecting.
Uninspiring.
Heartless.
Glacial.
Hostile.
Unfeeling.
Inimical.
Emotionless.
Passionless.
Apathetic.
Indifferent.
Insane.
Crazy.
Lunatic.
Raving.
Deranged.
Frantic.
Rabid.
Frenzied.
Reckless.
Perilous.
Senseless.
Unsafe.
Enraged.
Irate.
Furious.
Provoked.
Forgotten.

Mad from the Morning Light

Waking only to hear the screams. Knowing deep inside they pass from my own lips. Tasting fear from deep inside myself. Not remembering how I became this way. They look upon me as if I were a monster. Running from the morning sun, knowing it alone will show my true form. Knowing nothing will change the raw and bleeding emotions I have long ago forgotten how to feel. Wishing now I could change the horrendous creature I have become. A creature of my own making. Weak from listening to your words to me. I hear the words you whisper as I pass you in the night. You call me mad. You call me revolting and detestable. I hear the whispers as I lower my eyes from you. In the midnight hours, I feel whole and complete. The blackest of night is the only thing that can pacify my misery. Do not try to soothe my sorrow. The anger and anguish that I feel can never be understood. I do not wish the void to be filled. I do not feel anything other than pain. Perhaps soon, I will suffocate on the hatred I feel inside my soul. Soon I will be incinerated and truly be free of the anguish I feel. Perhaps it is true that I am raving and deranged. Void of all but hatred and animosity. Perhaps soon, you shall see my true form and quiver at my feet like the cowardly dog that you are. One day soon I can promise you will fear what I truly have become. None shall look upon my misshapen face and not feel true and authentic dismay. For when you look upon my true form, you shall only see your greatest fear staring back at you. Your own reflection.

Letter to My Son

I am writing you this letter as I watched you grow day by day. Your childish innocence is one I wish I could remember. I watch the way you enjoy the world around you. Everything new is exciting to you. When you discovered colors for the first time, I was there to see your smile. When you took your first step, I felt one day closer to the time you walked down the aisle at your graduation. When you first said Mommy, I felt a joy like I have never experienced in my life. Now that you are older, I watch you find the person you will someday become. I see how the simple things make you happy and how the tragedies in the world go unnoticed. As you grow day by day, I silently pray that you will never lose your inquisitive nature. I pray that you will remain true to yourself and learn life at your own pace. Don't stop and call the grass green because someone tells you it is green. Call the grass green and the sky blue because that is how you see it. Don't ever lose you childish innocence that is so precious. Hold on to what you believe and never be afraid to speak your mind. Never let others tell you that your thoughts don't matter. Always stand up for what you believe in. Always know that it's okay to cry. When you experience something for the first time. Always remember you did it on your own. Never doubt that you are right but always be willing to admit when you are wrong.

As you make your way through this tedious world, always remember the simple things in life. The smell of rain in the summertime. The feel of the sun as it warms your skin. The sound of the wind as it passes by your ear. Always remember what it felt like to taste something for the very first time. Remember who your friends are and always try to be friends to those who don't know how to ask to be your friend. Remember, even though it seems life has given you lemons, remember you learned early in life how to make lemonade. When you fall in love for the very first time, remember there will always be pain. But also, that there would be no love if you didn't first feel the pain.

There will always be bumps in the road but remember that the path that is worth walking is one you chose on your own. You are your own person and never let anyone tell you different. Don't let others tell you that you are meant to be seen and never heard. But remind others you are meant to be heard and seen as the individual that you are. Remember the happy times almost always fall between the sad times. Loved ones will come and go from your life. Tears will fall from your eyes. A good friend is someone that is there to see you through. To be a good friend, you are there always.

As you grow day by day, I am amazed to see the beauty you find in the smallest of things. The sound of a car starting can make you smile. Eating ice cream on a hot July day is something you find enjoyable. The day will come with you will learn what evil is. I hope that when it happens, you know that you are wise enough to walk away. Even though there will be times you want to give up, I hope that you will see it through until the end. When you feel that all the doors are closed and you've known where to go, you will always remember to try at least one more door.

There will come a day when you smile down at your own children, and I hope that I have taught you by then that children are special gifts from the heavens. They are meant to teach us. Not for us to teach them. Every day, I watch you go, and I learn more and more of what being a mother really is. There will come a time when you will fly from the nest you've so often called your home. When that day comes, know that I will always love you and be proud of the man that you've become. Know that you are my son and you've taught me as much I have can only hope to teach you. I hope you know that even when we are apart, you will always be inside my heart.

As I close this letter, I know there are things left unsaid. I know there are things you long to hear. I hope in time I'll have said them all. Just to see you smile, your innocent smile now is enough to know you've taught me enough lessons for today. In this walk of life, we do not choose our family. But in your heart, I hope you know. I would choose you from a million others because you are the missing piece of my soul.

Through the Rain

When I thought that it would rain forever, you came long and
Showed me the sun still makes rainbows. Just listening to the sound
Of your laughter causes me to smile. Never thought it was possible
To be this happy when I haven't even seen your face. You listen to me
When no one else seems to understand. You care about my pain.
You in your own way wipe away the tears. And make me see nothing
But rainbows and butterflies.

Until the day I met you, I carried a burden I thought would be
Forever in my soul. You make me forget about the past and focus
On the present. You let me show my inner child. My tears aren't out of
Anger anymore. They are out of joy. A joy so long ago forgotten. Until
You. Now I can see the light at the end of the tunnel. I can see the
Sun even when it's raining.

The rain has washed away the pain and given me a second chance.
I can start fresh and not be scared. Even though the thought of you makes
My heart pound in my chest and my head fill with unsaid things.
You truly are my rainbow after all the rain.

Breathing Easier

Today was a sunny day. But I was cold inside.
To everyone's eye, they could see me shivering.
Standing across from you made me sick. To see
that look in your eyes. To see how low you truly
were. Knowing deep inside you would kill me if
you could.

Every word you've ever said is a lie.
Every fist was supposed to be the last.
Every tear I cried I swore would be for something.
Everyone saw, but nobody tried to stop it.

The room filled with your hatred. You only
ever saw me as weak. But today I took my
stand. Today I put an end to the horror I
lived day by day. Today was the day that
I looked you in the eyes and called you a liar.

Every word you've ever said is a lie.
Every fist was supposed to be the last.
Every tear I cried I swore would be for something.
Everyone saw, but nobody tried to stop it.

From this day forward, you'll never touch
me again. From this day forward, the game
is at an end. I can breathe easier knowing
I took a stand. And I can see easier without
the haze of fear in my eyes. For you I feel
nothing but pity.

Borrowed Angel

Knowing that I'll never see your clear-blue eyes dancing with laughter again breaks my heart. Knowing that no one else will ever hear your laughter and see your magic smile leaves an empty void inside that nothing will ever fill. You were so young. You had your entire life to live, and it was taken away in one senseless act. People mourn your loss all over. Can't imagine tomorrow without you in it. You were the best friend I could have ever asked for. You accepted me for me. Never once did you stop to ask me to change. You laughed at my jokes when no one else understood them. Your arms held me when I cried. It was you I turned to when the world seemed to be spinning out of control. How do I say goodbye to a piece of my heart. A piece I know I can't live without. You were the friend I loved the most. Never intended on falling in love with you. Only to have you ripped out of my life so soon. Even though I know you'll never read this. Just know how much I miss you. God gave me an angel, and it seems it was time to take you home. I know you're safe from suffering, but I wish I could hold you just one more time. That's all I ask. I miss you so much. Just know you will always be in my heart. From now until forever.

The sound of your laughter will never be forgotten. The twinkle in your eyes will always be remembered. Whenever I feel alone, it's your arms I'll imagine around me. It will be your voice whispering to me when I am afraid. You are gone but never forgotten.

Joshua Daniel Andrews
October 29, 1979–October 24, 2005

Once my angel. Always my heart. Courageous warrior.
Loving brother, uncle, son, and soulmate.

You will forever be missed.

Here with Me Now

Walked outside this morning to a sky filled with gray and black. Haven't felt this empty in my life. Looking up to heaven to see if I can see you smiling down. Knowing that you are in a better place. I still miss your smile. I still miss your strong arms that held me until the demons went away. Looking at the sky wishing I could see you. Before my eyes, the clouds open, and a single ray of light shone down on me. I felt your hand caress my face. And heard your voice whisper to me. I am not there anymore little one. But I will never leave you. Remember me when you see the clouds and know that I am still here watching over you. It is my arms you slept in last night. Tears burned my eyes as the clouds gathered again and you seemed to fade away. But inside my heart, you will never fade. You will always be inside of me. You are gone, yes. But you will never be forgotten. Our love was one that knows no bounds. Even in death, we can't be separated. I look outside my window now and see the sun shining through the darkness. And I know deep inside you are here with me now. Here with me forever more.

In the Rain

Standing here alone in the rain. From the distance, I hear a sound that will forever haunt me.

I sole bugle sounds. Playing its heart-breaking song. Feeling the tears upon my cheeks.

Feeling pain tearing my heart into two. My entire body flinches at the sound of gunfire. Looking down, I see the small mass of people standing around a flag-covered casket. Do they know how beautiful the person inside was? How he could make you feel as if you're the only one in his life.

That his smile was one that stopped tears and hearts. The very presence of him overwhelmed you until you felt as if you could do anything. The bugle still sounds. It seems to echo off on the walls around us. As if we are inside of a box. A story that hasn't been told yet. And one that will make everyone that reads our story sob and ask the same questions we do. Why? Will they hear the sound of a lone bugle playing in their dreams? Will they wake up hearing a flag blowing in the wind? Will they even care? Does one's emotional distress cause others comfort when they feel they are alone? Does our story help any other lovers realize that their time is now? Because tomorrow is a mystery. Do they know that taking a leap of faith and putting your love and trust in someone is the safest and warmest feeling in the world? Will our memories go on once we are together again?

I look down again at the small mass of people. They are watching as the casket is slowly lowered into the earth. Can they feel you next to them like I do? Do they know that you were so special? That you loved life? That it was taken from you in one person's senselessness and another's error. How can they stand their crying when they didn't truly know you? How can they not feel your presence with them always? Keeping them safe. Why am I the only one left out in the rain alone in my sorrow?

With These Tears

With these tears, I wish to wash away your memory.
My heart hurts every time I'm near you. But I can't tell
you what is inside my heart. Not willing to risk losing you.
You are my angel in disguise. No one knows the reason
why we met. Only know that you held me when I cried.
When the world seemed to turn its back on me.
There you were telling me I could make it another day.
So wrap me in your wings again. Help dry these
tears that I can't seem to stop. Help me heal.
The pain I feel is tearing me apart. My sweet
angel. Help me with these tears.

Looking Glass

Standing in front of this mirror trying to find the real me. Never knowing which side of me I will see every day. Will it be the beaten side with no hope left? Will it be the mighty side that has no fears? How do others look at me as I pass them? They think I am weak. And I will hide in a corner. They don't know the many masks I hide behind. Masks that hide the true me. A me that no other has ever seen or will ever see. A private me that I work so hard to hide from the horrors of this wretched world. Every passing day, I stare at the objects on the counter. Trying to decide if it is worth it. Just to end this miserable thing I call life. Would it be worth it to leave this Earth by the use of the silver blade? Should I use something to make it quicker? Should I stare myself in the eye as I pull the trigger? Why is it I feel the walls closing in when no one else does? Am I the only one that feels completely alone in this world? In a room surrounded by people, I am alone. Standing in the sun, I am frozen. Sitting in a church, I am the only one without a soul. How is it my life became so meaningless? Was it the choices I made growing up? Is it the actions I create every day? How was I to know that my life would become an empty shell of existence? People's words ring hollow in my ears. All I hear from their truth is the hidden lies that speak. Why do I fear the mask I wear yet fear not wearing it more? Am I that different from the other people on this Earth that I feel I will not be accepted? Was it the battery I took in my youth? Where did the person I used to be go? Why does the world suddenly seem so lonesome? As I stare in the mirror in front of me, a deafening sound fills the air as the trigger is pulled. The meaningless life I once called my own slowly drains from the eyes in the mirror. The silver blade is forgotten. The mask I wore falls to the ground and shatters into pieces. I am left exposed and vulnerable. The sink in front of me fills with my crimson regrets. Never had a chance to tell the ones I loved the words I wished to say. In an instant, it was all taken from me. In one deafening sound, I was stripped of all that I knew and held dear. Disbelief stares back at me as I realize I didn't pull the trigger. Standing next to me are the people in this world I trusted most. They hold the smoking gun that has taken me away from this life. A life I didn't value until too late. Now I have nothing left. No breath left in my body. No blood left in my veins and no life left inside me. Those I trust stripped it all.

Inside the Tornado

Manic thoughts. Panicked thoughts. Someone dropped the marbles. Try to catch them before they all fall. Reaching, grasping, gasping for air. Spinning inside the tornado of life. Never knowing where you're going to land next. Or if you will ever really land. Mind goes numb from the long-downward spiral. Grasping for something to hold on to. Realizing that nothing can hold you down. Screaming at God asking him why He made you the way you are. Wishing someone could help it all end.

Manic thoughts. Panicked thoughts. Someone dropped the marbles. Spinning twirling hurling though space. Never stopped to see anyone's face. Screaming voices. Painful slaps. Hair tugs and people laughing. No one seems to see the pain that is so obvious. Yelling, telling. Asking why. Never understanding what it is that's going on.

Manic thought. Panicked thoughts. Hearing nothing around you but heart shattering shouts. Pain engulfs you. Taking away any feelings left inside. Not remembering where you started from. All you know is that somewhere you dropped the ball. Manic thoughts. Panicked thoughts. Someone dropped the marbles and you've lost them all.

Drowning

Standing in a sea of people, slowly drowning in the mass of chaos. Can't seem to find level ground no matter where I go. I try to cry for help, but the sounds of the busy street drown out the sound. Flailing hands waving to draw someone's attention. Burning fills my lungs as I am held under. Can't they see what they are doing to me?

Laying at the bottom of the ocean listening to the silence that greets me. No one was there to hold my hand. I slowly fell to the bottom of the pool. No one was there to keep me from losing my life. Pain is gone. Only sorrow is left. Couldn't they see I was screaming for help?

Were my words muted by the sound of sirens? Did the wind carry my voice away? How could they let me drown? All the times I was there in front of them, yet I was invisible. If I was so transparent, why couldn't they see I was bleeding inside? How was I left so alone? In a crowd so large how was I alone?

Now they question what they could have done differently? Should they have asked if I needed help? Should they have offered to stand by my side in my time of need? Now they feel the guilt setting in. Should they have been there for me? How could they have let me drown? One simply hand, and I would still be here today. How will they erase the guilt they feel?

Silver Blade

Count the marks on her arms. Were you blind to the blood that pours on your floors? Didn't you know she was bleeding from the touch of the silver blade? Was she cutting the pain away? Was she cutting in hopes she could remove the disappointment she carried around on her shoulders? Didn't you see how terrified she was of letting you down? All the time she asked what she had to do. And you left her alone. You told her she disgusted you. That you didn't know how you were supposed to love her?

All the marks from the silver blade. One for every time she disappointed you. One for every time she cried herself to sleep. How could you not see the marks? Did you hate her that much that you turned a blind eye to the crimson filling your white walls? Now you stand here asking how. How she could have embarrassed you this way. She shattered your picture-perfect life with her death.

Do you lie awake at night wishing you had listened more? Do you cry when you look at pictures of her? Did she even mean anything to you? Tearing her room apart, you find the blades. Hundreds of silver blades that marked your child's perfect skin. All the times you bragged about her at your tea parties. Never once did you ask her if she was okay. Instead, you saw but never heard.

The screams, they haunt you now. The pills still lay on the floor where she dropped them. Blood still stains your perfectly white floors. Do you even feel pain that she's gone? Do you realize you were blind to all the times she cried for you? Now you tell everyone you wish she would have found a different way. If only she had talked to you. Did you even listen to her? All the times she cried out at night for you.

Your perfect little angel wasn't so perfect. You put a burden on her that was too much to bear. The needles are scattered through her room. Empty vials in the drawer next to her bed. Still, you don't cry. Was she truly nothing more than a bother to you? All the years you pushed her off on other people. And yet you wonder why she didn't talk to you. Instead, you found her on the flood. With a pool of blood around her.

Blood now burned into your memory. Empty pill bottles in your box of memories. Vials still in her nightstand. Her room you've left as if a shrine to show how much you miss her. Yet you never saw the marks. You never saw the blood. You never noticed the silver blades. How could you be so blind? Your little girl is gone forever. And you're to blame.

Guilt

Standing in the center of the room as memories wash over me. I can still see the lights flashing. I can hear the screams from the people standing around. The rain forms a steady rhythm as it drops around us. Frozen with fear. Tears close off my throat. I want to reach out and touch you, but I know it's a memory. A memory of a night that changed my life. And as I fight the memory, I feel the guilt washing over me.

Leaving your side in your time of need is something that still haunts me. Hearing your voice in my head still forms a lump in my throat. Wish I could go back and change the hands of time. Pain like I've never felt before grips me. The tears still won't come.

Lying on the floor with the same sound on repeat. Images of the past flicker through my head. I can't remember your smile anymore. Or the sound of your voice. But I see the pain you left this world in. Wish I could have done more. Knowing it was hopeless.

The rain beats on the ground around me now. Ten years later and the guilt is still there. All the unanswered questions. Your face haunts me in my slumber. Knowing there was so much left unsaid. Emotions I couldn't say. That night still so fresh in my mind. Time hasn't dimmed a single detail.

Tears that rained from my eyes as they gave us the news. The pain that wrapped around me like a snake. Wanting to be there with you. Out of this world. Ten years of guilt still simmers under the surface. You were a friend. A brother and uncle; a son. All of that taken away in one man's drunken haze. Didn't even stop to see if he could help.

Voice screaming in my head. Pain weights my heart down. Tears form a lump in my throat. How does one deal with guilt they don't understand? Could I have done more? I miss my friend. I miss the petty fights. I miss the all-night laughter. I miss my defender. Most of all, I miss you.

So Long I

Now my arms feel empty because I ache to hold you. My lips feel sadness because they cannot touch yours. My heart still feels heavy with sorrow because we are so far apart. I want to climb the highest mountain and scream I love you for the world to hear. It's your face I see in my dreams. It's your arms I ache to be held in. Never realized what true love was until I met you. Now my heart is filled with sorrow and also with love and hope. Conflicted emotions. My tears I cry now are of pure joy. Your love for me fills my soul with hope. You truly are my angel in disguise. My prince waiting at the ball. Now I know what pure joy and true love really mean. Without you, I'd be hollow inside, and my heart would still be locked until the day you found the key.

Remembering How to Live

You know every day I wake up and ask the same question. Why do I still have to be here? I hate the way the world is. I hate the fact that everything has become about what you can buy, what you have, and how rich you and your friends are. Family values have been forgotten. Parents are more content with leaving their children in day care and with sitters. But then, they question why when their children stop talking to them about their day. They wonder why they are so distant and cold. I have a friend who's in love with a girl. So much so that he would go to hell and back for her. Yet she doesn't know it. I have a friend that is in a relationship that seems to be dragging him down and changing who he is. And I have to ask myself why I am still here in this hell. Then my son comes home with a childish love note. Dear Hunter, you are the cutest boy I know, and I am happy to be your girlfriend. Why is it so easy for children to say I love you and mean it? Why is it so hard for us? Children don't care what the other person has. Or how much they are worth. All they know is that, that person is always there. That is the real reason to live. Remembering that there are others in this world that still feel the way that we do. And watching children show *us* the real meaning of love and life.

Decade

Everyone says that time heals all wounds.
But I've had time, and inside, I'm still bleeding at the loss of you.
You were my friends. You made me smile. All the nights we'd stay up talking. Now a decade has gone past and I still expect to see you. I still miss the sound of your laugh. I miss the way you'd make me feel special.
You were a part of my life. A part that I can't let go.

Everyone tells me it's time to let go. To move on.
I've moved on. I've tried to put you out of my mind. But you still haunt me. The way we'd laugh over nothing at all. The nights we'd sneak away. And the adventures that we had. I have a hole inside of me that will never heal. I can't understand how I'm supposed to let go. When you're still with me every day.

You haunt my dreams. I hear you whisper in my eyes. When I feel alone you, hold my hand. People think it's time for me to forget. I never want to forget. You were my best friend. You were my first real friend.
Someone I could talk to. Someone that always tried to make me laugh.

Even when we fought, we'd end up laughing. Our fighting never went anywhere but in circles. I will always miss you. There are just some things time can't erase. And I'm glad that you are one of those memories. I will always hold you close to my heart.

Thank You

Every year, you watch the crowds and wonder why you even bother. No one cares what Christmas means. All they worry about is what is waiting for them under the tree. But every now and then, you see a miracle before your eyes. You find yourself standing in wonder as an angel in hiding passes by. When you feel you are at the end of your rope, someone comes along and throws you another to hang on to. When it seems the world is full of hatred, you find that one ray of light shining down on you. And the meaning of Christmas fills your soul. You see the reason you still believe that magic and still happen if you believe enough. During this Holiday season, you have shown me this. Your actions have humbled me. And you truly were sent to this family for a reason we may never understand. Even when your family has lost so much, you've found it in your heart to give to someone else. And you've helped show me that the meaning of Christmas isn't dead and gone. There will never be the right words to say to you and yours. Thank you doesn't seem to be strong enough. But you have showed me that angels do walk this earth. You simply have to pay attention because if you blink, you might just miss the one that is placed in your life at a time when you feel hopeless. You are raised to believe that good things happen to those who deserve it. Yet when something good does happen, you ask yourself what you did to deserve it. So, I ask myself this: How will I ever repay you for the kindness you have bestowed upon me? Thank you for showing me that goodness does still exist in this world.

How Is It Possible

How is it possible that the tiniest snowflake can make such a big impact on one's life? That the slightest ripple in the lake you're staring at can cause ripples in your life? And how is it possible that before you know it, another year's gone by, and you're still where you were a year ago? Standing in the very same spot. Staring at the very same lake. Watching the very same ripple? Did you miss the door that you should have walked through? Did all your dreams come crashing down around you like a hailstorm? Leaving bruises that just seem they will never heal?

How is it possible for one to bleed inside and no one knows? Can't they see the pain in your eyes? Didn't they hear your shattered heart crying out for comfort? How is it one can be so alone in a world so full of people? How is it possible to be in love one day, and the next, it's gone from your life? Did you even get to say goodbye? How is it possible to be with so many friends yet be so disappointed? Didn't you realize they would disappoint you? Didn't you know that the only person to trust is yourself?

Is it possible to realize that the one thing you thought you wanted more than your next breath was the wrong thing? And that the most unexpected diamond has been hidden in the rough right in front of you? Can you gather the courage to take one more chance? Can you grasp the hand that's been stretched toward your drowning soul the whole time? Is it possible to find an angel waiting patiently for you to say their name?

Grandfathers

Grandfathers are there to be loud and gruff. But they are still there when things are rough. They tell you stories that help you learn about that past. You learn so much from their stories of days long gone. Sometimes, they seem so mean. But underneath is a heart that is true and clean. They teach you what your parents have done. And help you see that you're just like one. Sometimes, they seem so old. But other times, they seem like laughing kids. Grandfathers are strict and stern. But without them, there are things we'd never learn. And even as a young child, you learn to love them for who they are. Never in your entire life did you ever expect to miss them so much. Even when they are still here with you. Making you laugh and smile. There is a piece of you that is secretly always wishing that they didn't have to go. But inside, you know their part in history is coming to an end. They've taught you all you need to know from them. Stories of their early days make you laugh and bring you joy. Spending time near them makes you warmer than standing in the sun. Because a grandfather's love is something you never forget. Even when the time comes when things get tough. You remember the lessons your grandfather has taught you. You learn at a young age to be proud of where you come from. You learn when you're small that to carry the name you do is something to be proud of and hold you head high. You learn many of life's lessons from their tales of days long past. Stories of war, of marriage, of job long gone. Stories of children you never dreamed could be like you. You learn the way they loved their children. And your grandfather helps you see your parents in a different way. They are no longer strangers without a past. You know their secrets and the mischief they wrought. Spending time with your grandfather can mean more to them than you will ever know. Because you never take the time to learn. They have history that you should be eager to learn. Grandfathers don't always show their love. They grew up in a time where emotions weren't for men to show. But in their own ways. In subtle ways, they show their love. In things they make you. In stories they tell you. The way they hug you when you think you're alone in the world. But a time comes when your grandfather doesn't remember you. He doesn't remember the smiles he caused you. He doesn't remember the stories he's told. There comes a time when your grandfather isn't there anymore. And at that time, you have to look back at all the joys and all the love he's shown you. And even if he calls you by a different name. Or if he remembers everyone but you. You know in your heart that he'll always be a part of you. His stories will help keep him alive in your heart. His rules will be something you miss when you least expect it. And when you grow old, you will hope to be just like your grandfather who was strong and defiant. Marching to a tune all his own. And never let a day go by that you don't thank God that He gave you the grandfather that He did. The things you learned from him are memories you'll keep forever. So don't be sad when your grandfather goes away. Remember him the way he was, loud and gruff. By being there when things were tough. That will keep him alive inside your heart. Until the day you pass. To my grandfather, I hope you know just how special you are to me. I will forever hold the memories of you deep inside my heart.

Hunter's Birthday Letter

I can still remember the first time I felt you kick inside my stomach. It filled me with wonder and with awe. That I could be carrying one of God's angels inside of me. I never asked questions like *why me*. All I could say was thank you for giving me one of your angels. I remember humming to you before you were born. I remember telling the world I was having a boy. In my mind, I pictured baseball games and dirty hands. Not to mention all the scraped-up knees for me to kiss.

The day you were born was the best day of my life. Until you were in my arms, you didn't seem real. I looked down at your tiny little hands and your wrinkled little face and remember feeling a lump in my throat because you're here before me. In my very own arms was a gift from God. My beautiful son.

The first time you smiled at me, I felt my heart flip over. I couldn't be prouder than I was the day you smiled at me. I would hold you to me and hum a nameless tune that later became Hunter's tune. I would rock you in my arms and know I was holding an angel.

Over the years, we've had so many happy times. But we've also had times where you've been sick and scared. I've been there the best I could be. Holding you to me wishing I could take your fears away. But I know now that these past seven years have been a blessing that I would never wish to take back.

Now that you're seven, there is still so much to see and learn. There are more baseball games and days at the park. Summer nights filled with catching bugs. And lazy summer days of catching fish and spending time together. Watching ice cream melt over your hands and knowing I have a mess to clean.

But now that you're seven and you have your own personality, I can only smile with fondness and remember the early days. The time you said your first word. The first time you crawled. The day you took your first step. Before my very own eyes you grew up. Now, you are no longer my little boy. Because now, you are my little man. And I couldn't be prouder than I am every time I look at you. You are my heart and soul. And I hope that someday, you can look back at this and smile. Happy birthday, Peach. I love you.

A Thank-You to a Soldier

There are no words that can express the thanks that you deserve. You fought in a battle that not many understood, and you faced challenges that no one can comprehend. You remained silent when you were scared. The amount of thank-yous that you deserve will never come close to equal all the loss that surrounded you. I know there are times you sit and wonder why you fought for this country when it never even repaid the debt it owes. It has been said that freedom comes with the highest price. And for those who have fought in a battle and know that statement is true. We thank you. It should not be on holidays that you are thanked. It should be every day of free living that you are. That your fallen brothers are remembered. That when asked what freedom is, children should be able to answer that it is something that was earned and not something that was given. Our country has become a country that takes its liberties for granted. No one says thank you. No one salutes soldiers or the flag. People protest wars then whine when they lose freedom. They don't stop to ask if their neighbor lost a son or daughter. So on this day of memory, I wish to say thank you for being a solider. And thank you for the freedom you fought so hard to preserve for a nation that does not truly appreciate it. You lost friends. You lost family. And today I say thank you for the beliefs you fought so hard for.

Reflections

They say that a photograph captures part of one's soul. If that is true, what of one's reflection? Does the reflection feel the pain we feel? When you touch the mirror, the image is solid but hollow. There is no feeling in the reflection.

Reflections mimic our expressions. If we cry, they cry. If we smile, they smile. Wouldn't it be nice if for once they could carry our pain and emptiness for a while? Take the burden from our shoulders and let us feel free for the first time since childhood.

Reflections are simply a shadow with more defined features. There is no hope of outrunning the pain we feel when we look in a mirror. There is no changing who we are. The reflection gives it all away.

Hollow Heart

I hear your soft cries echoing around me everywhere I go. The smell that would have been your own was harshly ripped away. My arms seem hollow and broken. They ache to hold you in them. No one knows that feelings that go around inside me.

I never got to hold you. I only dreamed of holding you. Of counting ten perfect toes and fingers. My dreams are now empty. There is no reason to dream now. I'll never hear your first cry, or see you take your first breath. I'll never feel you moving or kicking all about. All my dreams were harshly yanked away from me.

They pat your back and hug you. But they left you all alone. Where were they when I lost you? They left me all alone. These tears I wish would fall. Only seem to weigh me down. I wish I could just hold you. But you're in a better place now. You're my little angel. Sitting next to God. I will see you one day. Today was just not my day.

Blind Eye

Has anyone noticed that over the years, people have become blind to what the words *love, trust, honor, respect, friendship,* and *family* truly mean? I mean look at it this way. When is the last time you willingly gave something up for someone else without complaining? When is the last time you put your life on hold to be there to help someone? To care for an elderly relative? Has the world become so consumed by what they want that they can't see who they are hurting? Love? What is it really? In the dictionary, it says that love means strong affection, warm attachment, attraction based on sexual desire, a beloved person, unselfishly loyal and benevolent concern for others, cherished, to feel passion, caress, to take pleasure in. Yet we've cheapened love to mean nothing more than a four-letter word we use when we want something. And Trust? Here's it's real meaning: assured reliance on the character, strength in someone or something, basis of reliance, faith, hope, confident hope. Yet once again, we've taken that and twisted it to fit us. Honor. Does anyone even know what that even means anymore? Honor: free from deception, trustful, genuine, reputable, marked by integrity. Yet here is something we take for granted every day. We forget about all of the men and women fighting a never-ending battle for our freedom. Defending our honor or lack thereof. Respect: to consider deserving of high regard, yet we turn our heads from all the fighting going on in the world. We bicker over what to call Christmas, or if we are even allowed to say anything along those lines. Friendship: one attached to another by affection or respect, one who supports of favors someone, one who is not hostile. Yet here we are again, turning on friends for simple mistakes. And Family: a group of people living in one household of the same blood or difference of blood. A group of people that are there when one member is lost or hurting. Yet we spit on our family's faces every day. So this poses the question: Do we truly know what anything of value is anymore? Is it simply what one can buy us? Is it simply what one thinks of us? Should we change to fit into everyone else's mold? And why is it so hard for us to say I love you to someone, but I hate you seems so easy? Why is it harder to commit oneself to a project that is useful to others then to help an ailing family member? How can we call ourselves human when we are the way we are?

Dream Come True

Waking from a peaceful slumber wishing you could hold on to the prince from your dream. He fought dragons and evil wizards to protect you. Every time his blue eyes looked your way, you felt your heart miss a beat. He is everything you wanted him to be. And now, you fight to hold on to his memory.

The sound of his sweet voice haunts you as you move through the day. All you hear is his sweet voice whispering I love you. Three words you've dreamed of since you were a little girl. You feel an ache deep inside that no one but your prince can fill. An ache that won't ever go away.

You lay awake at night wishing to dream of him. Begging for your dreams to come true. Rolling over, you see your lover lying next to you and realize your prince has been with you always. Your dreams came true the day you said I do. And he will be with you forevermore.

Are You with Me?

Feeling hollow. Darkness all around me. Listening to the ticking of the clock on the wall. Sadness fills my soul. And emptiness I cannot name creeps through me. How can I be called human when I feel as if I'm a ghost? Can't you see the pain I'm in? Are you blind to the misery I live in? Since you went away my soul left me also. I once told a tale of a River. I once told a tale of Borrowed Angels. But now in this moment I am alone.

If I pulled this trigger, would anyone hear the sound? If I drove this knife into my heart, would anyone miss my laughter? I am hollow. Are you with me? Would you see me if I pulled this trigger? Would you stop the silver blade from cutting my skin? The knife buried deep in my chest, would you stop the bleeding? Are you still with me? Every time I see a star, I think of you? I hear a bell, and I think of you? Are you here with me? If I wanted to join you, would you let me? Am I too young? Do I have too much left to do? Are you here?

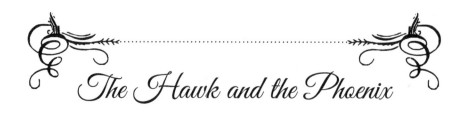

The Hawk and the Phoenix

There is a tale of the hawk and the phoenix. The hawk has sharp eyes and keen senses. It could hunt and provide for its family. It was a mighty warrior. The hawk was held in the highest esteem. All of the birds wanted to be the hawk. The hawk held his head high as he scouted the grounds below him for prey.

The tale of the phoenix is not so grand. It was not held; it is the highest regard. Though the phoenix was a fighter. She fought for everything she had. Her family. She laid her life on the line time and time again. It is said that when a phoenix dies, she rises from the ashes stronger than before.

One day, the hawk found the phoenix lying on the ground bleeding from a hunter's arrow. The hawk looked into the phoenix's eyes and swore to her he would protect her. Nothing would happen to her. The phoenix merely smiled and told him. She didn't need protection. She would be fine. Before his eyes, the phoenix vanished.

Months went by and still, the hawk replayed that day over in his head. How had she simply vanished? She was one of the most stunning animals he'd ever seen. And she vanished into thin air. The hawk landed by the river and sighed. "Don't sigh, my brave hawk. I am here," a voice whispered. The hawk turned and found his phoenix. Whole and glowing in the ray of orange and red flames. "I will always return to you, my hawk. For this is where my heart is," the phoenix said softly. The hawk watched as she flew into the distance, and that is the story of the hawk and the phoenix.

End Times

Reaching, screaming, begging for mercy. Is this what we have to look forward to? Wailing, shouting, cursing at those who didn't offer help. Is it truly their faults we didn't listen? We sit in flames in hell and wonder why we are here. When in the back of our minds, we know. They tried to help us. And we scuffed at them. The time your mother asked you to go to church with her, you were too busy. The time your friend asked you to listen to a verse they were reading, you laughed at them. All the times someone asked you to pray with them for the men and women overseas fighting for your freedom, you said prayer won't do it. Now you sit here in hell surrounded by flames and wonder why.

Sitting up in bed gasping for air. Sweat soaks your body. Your dream still fresh in your mind. You run through the house waking everyone. Telling them you need to pray. That there are men and women, mothers and fathers, brothers, and sisters. Sons and daughters fighting a war not just for our country but also for our souls. Not just overseas. But in our own backyards. Now is the time to realize. We can make a difference. It's not too late. It's not the end of times.

Misunderstood

I went to school today, and the same groups of kids all laughed and stared. One day, soon, I will show them how wrong they are. I'm more than an outcast. I am more than a child from a broken home. I have more to offer than to be the butt of their joke. One day soon, they will all learn.

Months go by and they still laugh and stare. My plan goes on as I ignore their stares. The cheerleaders who are all vain and worry about their looks. The jocks that all have the nerds do their work so they make the grade so they can play. The Science geeks that are always working on something new. Soon they will all learn.

Graduation day is the day they will remember who I am. They call my name, and lo and behold, the entire school is looking around to see who I am. I am the quiet one that never spoke. I am the one who turned in their homework on time every day. I am the one that graduated with honors. And I am the one that has been misunderstood my entire time in school. So as I give this speech, I ask all of you to look at the person next to you and think: Do you truly know anything about them?

Crimson Regret

Standing over my lifeless body watching my crimson regret pool around on the floor. No one here to stop the flow of all the mistakes I made pour out of my veins. The pain I suffer is no longer here. I see the light shining so bright and beautiful calling my name. Looking down again at the pool of crimson regret lying on the floor. No tears are in my eyes. No sorrow is felt. No emotion seems to be present as I stare at my lifeless body in the pool of crimson on the floor.

Below me, I hear the commotion. My family screaming for the medics to hurry. They don't realize I don't feel any pain any longer. The manic thoughts are gone. The fine line of bipolar is over. It's spilled on the floor in a pool of crimson. I watch the medics try to stop the flow, but it's too much.

At the hospital, I stare at my lifeless body connected to countless monitors. They push air into my lungs. They fill my veins with fresh blood. Family and friends come and go. Tears fall from their eyes, and they whisper they knew this would happen. I wasn't strong enough. I wasn't stable enough. Sooner or later, I would take the blade to my wrist and try to cut out the pain. Looking closely, I see a flicker of life in my body. My eyes begin to twitch. I know it's time to end my journey. I walk to the bed and lay on the body in the bed and the sounds around me fade. The images of the crimson stay vivid on my mind. I found a way to bleed my pain out. A pain no one else would ever understand.

Everyone whispers behind my back. They act like I can't hear the things that they are saying. They are waiting for me to hurt myself. They think that I can't handle the amount to stress I am under. They see my being bipolar as a curse. I see it as a blessing. Yes, there are black-letter days. But there are also days where I am so happy and creative that I wish I would never come down from the natural high that I was on.

Standing over my lifeless body. Watching my crimson regret spill all over the floor. Hoping that everyone will one day understand that it was their words. Their treatment. Not my choice. I didn't get here alone. They helped put the razor in my hand. They helped spill my crimson regret.

Untold Secret

Second tick by as my mind drifts off. Images of you flow through my mind. Every time I've seen you smile is burned into my memory. The sound of your voice is something I hold close to my heart. It's your arms I wish held me at night. Every time I see you, I wish I could tell you this secret I hold deep inside. These feelings that swim around inside of me every time I think of you.

Watch the flames of the candle dance and think of you. Wishing you were here with me. Wishing I could tell you how your smile makes me feel. How just the sound of your voice makes me melt. Knowing that this is a secret I will hold deep inside. Your eyes they fill my dreams and make me ache for things I am unaware of ever wanting before.

Deep inside knowing I've never felt this way before. Every moment of the day is filled with thoughts of you. Dreaming of you. Wishing you were the one that held me through the night and kept me safe. Your voice sends shivers through my body. Your eyes are so warm and welcoming. Wishing I could just tell you this secret that I hold.

Don't want to keep this a secret anymore. What would you say if I told you how I felt? Would you tell me you felt the same? Would you laugh and walk away? So many uneasy emotions swimming inside of me. Not knowing what to do or say. So I simply smile and laugh when you are near. But inside, I am slowly breaking to pieces. You're my secret. One I wish I could tell.

Locked Inside

Locked inside a box hidden so far away. No one knows what secrets it holds only that its wonders must be great. Is it letters of dying lovers' last requests? Or is it merely trinkets from one's past?

Locked inside my secret box are my memories of your smile and your eyes. The way they seem to dance when you smile and the sound of your laughter. For me, my secret box is far more valuable than any amount of silver or gold. For every time I open my box, I find a tiny piece of you.

Memories that I wish to hold are forever locked inside my box. And the key in a place that no one will ever think to look. My secret is safe with me. Until my dying day. The times I open the box, I see your smiling face. I ache to feel your warm embrace. I dream of you every night when I close my eyes. You are a phantom that haunts me through the all the moments of my day.

Inside, I am slowly bleeding. I want to show the world, the beauty, and wonder of the secrets inside my secret box, but I know that once I do, I can't take it back. And I'd rather have you in my fantasy than never have you at all. So at night, I see in the candlelight watching how it casts an eerie glow over the tiny box in my hands. Slowly, I open the lid and let my secret out. My feelings for you come pour out. No longer a secret and no longer inside this tiny box.

Long Lost Words

Long lost words I never dreamed I'd ever say again swim through my heart. Every beat brings them closer to the surface. Seeing rainbows wherever I look. And I look at the world with a new light. A burden has been lifted from my shoulders with a simple smile from you. All this time, I have hidden from the possibility of falling in love, and yet, here I stand. On the ledge ready to fall. Arms extended. Seeing the world brighten before my very eyes.

For months, you have consumed my thoughts. Your voice brings a smile to my face. The mere thought of you can turn my darkest day into a luminous joy-filled day. I don't know how it happened or when. But these long-lost words are begging for me to let them out. But I still hold back out of fear. Fear that you will not return them. Fear that it is too soon.

Months of tossing and turning. Months of dreaming of only you have brought me to this ledge. Teetering on the edge. Do I fall, or do I walk away? Should I let the colors embrace me? The warmth I feel consume me? Or shall I walk away? Long-lost words I fear the most now swimming in my mind every day. Finally feel fixed after years of being broken.

Your smiles give me the strength to go on. The thought of you helps me continue through the day. Wake up from this dream and realize that yesterday should have been the day I told you those long-lost words. Is it too late?

Eraser

Is it too late to go back in the past and erase the mistakes of my past? Did you know that broke up my family? Do you know that there are some in my family that really hate me? Can't I please have an eraser? I want to erase the mistakes from my past and fix my family.

Fighting in every room that you walk into. Screaming that never seems to dull inside your head. Anger that simmers around you. Mistakes that can never be taken back. Fighting that never ends. Is there an eraser somewhere I can use? I just want to fix my family.

Never knew a child could be to blame for the mistakes of a family. The fighting that continues over the years being placed on their shoulders. An uneasy peace left to rest in one's hands. Are there any erasers large enough to erase the pain I feel?

Did you know I broke up my family? That I should be responsible for the end of our family. My mistakes were too much for my family to bear. I am the one that caused the fights. I'm the reason that people turned against one another.

Forgive me for the mistakes I've made. Can't we find an eraser to take the mistakes away? Can't we push the pain and anger aside and work on being a real family? Why is it my shoulders that the responsibility rests on? Is there an eraser large enough to rid this family off all the mistakes I made?

In Your Arms

In your arms, I found heaven. The rays shine down on me each time you smile. Your blue eyes set my soul on fire. My heart beats a new beat. A beat it's never felt before. In your arms, I feel loved and protected. And when your lips brush mine, it sends shivers down my spine. Feeling a love I cannot put into words. When you are not here, I feel half alive.

In your arms, I feel I can face my fears for the first time. A warmth surrounds me that I never want to fade away. When you whisper my name in such a tender tone, every fiber of my soul melts knowing this is the one.

In your arms, all my nightmares fade. You are part of my strength. You are part of me. I want to spend forever in your arms. Knowing that together, we can chase away the rain. If I came to you and told you I loved you, would you run away? Or would you let me stay?

In your arms, I see forever. I know we'll have our hard times. But I know that as long as you keep holding me in your arms. We'll get through them. I know that over time, we'll have our joys. And that's a dream I want to believe.

I want to wake every morning in your arms. I want to fall into a sated slumber in your arms after our passion has burned itself out for the night. In your arms is where I want to be. Today, tomorrow, and forever. If I told you I loved you, would you run away? Or would you let me say?

Lost

You used to be the shoulder I cried on. It was you that would take away my pain. Through the years, you've been my rock. Now you aren't there anymore. One fight. One misunderstanding. One angry conversation. And you are gone. Do you feel the same pain I feel? Are you as empty as I am? Does it feel as if your heart has shattered and will never be whole again?

So many memories I hold inside. The way we used to laugh until we cried. The times we just sat in silence because words weren't needed between us. The way your arms held me when no one else would. Now I am falling, and you aren't there to catch me. Do you feel the same pain?

The words said in anger can never be taken back. The bleeding inside can never be taken away. The saying "sticks and stones" is so untrue. Words hurt more than fists. They wrap around your soul and rip it to pieces. Does it feel as if your heart has shattered and will never be whole again?

These tears can't seem to stop falling. My heart can't stop hurting. My best friend is gone. My rock is now turned to dust. The arms that used to hold me when I was hurting are no longer open. Are you as empty as I am?

Don't you know how much you mean to me? How much our time together means to me. Our stupid conversations that seem to go in circles. The things we've been through together bonding us forever together. The way we used to hold each other's hearts. Do you remember those times? Do they even still matter?

Is this all now lost because of words said out of anger? Words said out of spite? Tell me what I have to do to make us whole again. My world doesn't exist without you in it. We used to be two halves of a whole. Now we are nothing more than drifters in the wind. Does it matter that your words hurt? Do you care that you're the cause of these tears? Have you forgotten the promises we made to each other? Now you are lost to me forever. And I feel so alone.

Once Again

    Should have listened to the whispered words around me. Knew this dream was too good to be true. Instead, I chased the impossible dream. I believed that love truly did exist for me. Now I'm wishing I could stop the pain that is filling every breath I take. Nothing seems to numb this pain I feel inside. As if a million razors run over my skin. Spilling my blood around me. Am I too lost to be saved? Still my heart betrays me as it beats for you. These tears I cry are for you. I try to tell myself that you're gone. That you've left me. That I was left alone. Yet my heart doesn't want to believe. How could I have fallen in love if I was going to be left alone again? The wall I built was so strong. Yet here I stand broken hearted. Bleeding inside. And once again. All alone.

In a Glass Globe

Standing in the center of a glass globe watching the world go on around me. Sounds are muffled. No one can hear my cries but me. I feel alone in this world. Shattered heart lying at my feet. No one to help me pick up the pieces. Did you know if you shake me, pieces fall like snow?

Whispered words I hear around me. Secrets kept from me so that I'm not hurt. Yet here I lay bleeding inside with no one to stop to flow. Wish to God I could break the glass that surrounds me. But I know I am forever trapped in this world of solitude.

Is that an angel I see smiling down at me? The light around him so bright and blinding. Begging him to help me piece together the shards of my broken heart. But no one knows where the glue is. Can it even be mended? Am I truly alone in this world?

Did you know if you shake this globe I'm in, pieces fall around me like snow? Silently and slowly. Muffling all the cries of pain I have. No one sees my tears. No one hears my pleas. I am alone in this glass globe.

Nightmare

Every time I close my eyes, I see you laughing. I hear your voice. No matter how loud I scream, the torture never ends. Every night, I relive the hell you put me through. Tears only made you angry. They made your hits harder. In my nightmares, you're still standing over me with a blade to my throat. Screaming. In the distance, I hear my innocence dying. Begging for him to stop hurting me.

Every night I close my eyes, it's your face I see. As if the player is stuck on repeat. I can't make the memories go away. The scaring is on the inside where no one sees it. Everyone thinks I am happy all the time. No one knows the hell I lived through. The images that haunt me. The blood pooled around me on the floor. The mascara streaming down my face.

You laugh and joke with friends. Telling them it was an easy score. That I wanted it as much as you did. What you didn't tell them when how hard I fought. That the claw marks on your face were from me fighting to protect myself. That I begged and begged and all you did was laugh. Does that make you more of a man? Because you killed someone's innocence? Didn't you hear her screaming? Didn't you hear her dying?

Now it's all a nightmare that I live every night. One that will never go away. Images of blood, pain, and anger. Deep inside, I know my innocent side is gone. And you're all to blame.

As You Slumber

Sitting here at this late hour. Watching the rise and fall of your chest as you sleep in peaceful slumber. Do you ever dream of me? Am I alone in this feeling? Restless wakefulness fills my veins. My only peace comes from watching you sleep. Knowing that you are at peace and rested. My heart seems to forget how to beat as I remember the feel of your arms around me. It's been so long since you just held me. Never realized how much I missed that feeling until this fitful night. Now I sit here and watch you slumber. I often wonder, *What is this weakness inside of me I feel every time I'm near you? Why does my heart beat a different beat? Why does my body seem to tingle with just a smile from you?* A simple look from your eyes sets my soul on fire. I sit and watch you breathe and feel as if my soul is linked with yours. For every time you breathe, there is a hold inside of me where my heart should be. And only you can fill that space. So as you lie in slumber, do you ever feel me near? Do I cross your dreams? Watching the rise and fall of your chest as you slumber. Knowing deep inside there is no other for me then you. Never have I found such peace in watching someone sleep. As my eyes grow heavy, it's your face that dances through my dreams. Am I alone?

Angel of Death

As I lie here begging for death to take me, memories of my life flicker like a silent film through my head. My body grows colder as each memory passes. Wish I could have changed this outcome but knowing deep inside that nothing would be different even if I'd said the words I felt sooner. Nothing would be different. I'd still be lying here with this crimson pool around me. These pills would still be scattered on the floor from the dropped bottle. Tears roll down my frozen cheeks. Not even their warmth can change the feelings I have coursing through my body. I wish I could be the one that made you happy. I would have given anything and everything to be what you needed me to be. But instead, you left me for another. Now I lie here bleeding, waiting for these pills to stop my heart. The pain is too much for me to take. Wish like hell, the angel of death would just come and tell me my time is now. That I can go with him. What is taking him so long? He has taken so many from me, but this time, I ask him to take me. He does not show? Am I meant to suffer for all of my days? Alone in this cruel world? The pain is becoming too much to bear. Please, angel of death, I beg you. Stop these memories flashing in my head. Stop this shattered heart from beating another beat. Take me now. I want this to be over. I don't want to remember the love I had for him that was coldly rejected and tossed aside. I don't want to remember that I wasn't good enough. I don't want to remember that I'm not loveable. Please take me now! I beg of you! Angel of death, take me now!

My Brian

Long summer days filled with laughter and jokes. Short winter days filled with snowball fights and football games. That's what I remember about my Brian. The trouble we used to get into and the fun we used to have. The pranks we used to play and the laughs we used to have. The tears we cried together over loses that we shared. Nights of sneaking out and laughing. All the crazy things we used to do. The bonfires we used to have and the fireworks we used to shoot. Endless summers filled with days of swimming and sitting around. Old commercials that we used to laugh at. And the old music we used to play. Sitting in your room looking out the window talking about the future. And all the things we wanted to do. You're the only one that ever pulled off a real surprise party for me. That's what I remember about my Brian. Chasing each other around over stupid things. Fighting over football games. Watching *Super Bowl* together and having our own parties where no one was allowed but us. Two cousins together like siblings and best friends. Where you found one, you found the other. Paper-route duty during the summer, and the oldies dance in your backyard. Hiding from crushes in your basement while you told me if they were gone or not. That's what my Brian did for me. I remember the day you were bit by the dog on your paper route. The endless games of cards we used to play. And the dare to walk through the park at night. Never letting on that I was terrified, but you held my arm the whole time knowing I was scared. That's how my Brian was with me. Yes, we went our separate ways growing up. But we still tried to stay close. The times we spent together felt like there were no lost time in between. You were my Brian. You made me laugh. You made me cry. There were days you made me so mad I couldn't see straight. But that is what cousins do. We were closer than cousins. You were my best friend growing up. My partner in crime. Always there beside me when I was in trouble. We spent a summer seeing just how much trouble we could cause.

The cops on the fourth of July. Sneaking out every night. Hanging out playing games and listening to music. That was my Brian. I know we grew apart, but you will always be in my heart. I hope you know I loved you. You were my best friend growing up. You helped me through my embarrassing moments. You covered for me when I was in trouble. Thank you for being there for me all those years. That's how I'll remember my Brian. And how I hope the rest of the world will remember you too. The Brian that laughed at everyone's jokes. The Brian that was there to lend a hand. How we used to make your Dad so mad every summer when he was working in the front yard. How we used to hide the Browns helmet. And laugh when your Dad would rant and rave. How we'd tease your Mom about her early morning sales. And find a million ways out of them. That was my Brian. And I hope the world remembers that smile. And the way your eyes would twinkle with mischief. I'm sorry for the time we lost. But you'll never stop being my Brian. The cousin I grew up with. My best friend. RIP, Brian. Know that you were loved and are going to be dearly missed.

September 17, 1982–February 28, 2008

Voids

All the times I cried, you were never there. Every time you said I promise, you broke another piece of my soul. Now your words fall on deafened ears. Anger and rage fill me now. Times when I needed you the most, you turned your back on me. Left me standing in the cold and rain alone and broken. I love you and I promise are eight letters. So is bullshit. And that is all I hear now. You've killed my faith in love. You've destroyed my trust in men. Every time I hear the words I promise, I know there is another let down coming. You've never cared about the successes in my life. Unless I was messing up, you didn't want anything to do with me. You told lies about me behind my back. You showed false concern. Everyone says look beyond the past. Find a positive in the pain. No one knows the anger I feel. No one understands the rage that boils beneath the surface. You tell the world I'm your little girl. I am nothing to you. You left me a long time ago. Every fall, I've taken you set me up for. Every dark path, I've walked you set before me. You lied to me. You told me you'd always be there for me. That you'd never let me down. You promised me. And made a fool of me when I believed you. Voids that will never be filled now seethe with anger. Now bleed with sorrow. You lied to me. You made a fool of me. You broke my spirit. I am forever broken because of you.

Fool Again

Lies everywhere I turn. Everything I thought to be true turned into dust before my very eyes. Realize now what a stupid fool I was to think you meant a word you said to me. Everything was a lie. I was a puppet to you, and you played with my strings and made me do your bidding. Now I see just how blind I truly was. Every time my heart told me not to listen, I turned away. Now I sit here with nothing more than a pile of dust in front of me. Waiting for a new wind to blow in and erase this misery from my life. Never should have listened to you. I was just a game you played when you were bored. Now my eyes are open, and I see just how much you used me. I never meant a single thing to you. Pretty words hid your lies. Like a witch with a poison apple, you stood before me. Tempting and appeasing to the senses. Now I'm left with nothing but self-doubt and self-hatred. I swore no one would ever hurt me again. No one would make me a fool again. Yet here I stand. A fool again.

Waiting for Me

I think of all the times that we will never have together. All the firsts that will never happen. All the words I will never hear you say. Tears they burn my eyes as your memory sears my mind. You are a part of me that I will never let go. I know you are above me now guiding me in my choices. And I feel you when I am at my lowest. When the wind blows gently, I smell your tender powdery scent. My arms ache to hold you. My lips still tremble as they form your name. How could someone so special and small be taken away before I could tell them how I felt? There is a void inside that will never be filled. Will this ache always hurt? Will I always feel so alone? I used to dream of what you would look like. I used to count the days until I held you. Now that day will never come. And I am left to ask myself what I did wrong. Could I have done something to change your fate? Every night as I lay my head on my pillow, I look at the sky and smile sadly knowing you are there waiting for me.

Living Hell

My skin feels like it's splitting. My heart is pounding in my chest. Finding it hard to breathe. Can't they find what's wrong with me and simply cut it out of me? Why do I have to live this way? In constant agony. Is it fair that everyone simply pats my hand and tells me it's okay? That all I need to do is forget my problems and my pain will go away? What would they do if they had to live my life? Could they handle living in my shoes for just one day? Would they crack under the pressures I withstand every day? This is a living hell I've tried so many times to leave. Tears are useless. Pain is endless. Yes, I know I am the same little girl I once was many years ago. But I am the same little girl that never had a chance to be that girl. I grew up too fast. I was forced to become someone of their design. Now I wonder why they can't see I'm not like this on my own. My skin is burning. My dreams are full of feverish nightmares. Dry mouth and aching head. Just want the pain to stop and let me rest a little. I will not revert to my old self. Not now that I've come this far. I will leave this living hell even if it kills me.

You Found Me

Alone so for so many years, I wasn't even looking when you first said hello. Never in my wildest dreams did I think in a matter of hours you could steal my heart. I laid awake at night reading our conversations over and over. Smiling at the sweet things you would say to me. And how you would laugh at even my stupidest joke. Never did I see it coming, and it scared me senseless that I fell so quickly. Terrified to say anything because I knew you'd never feel the same for me. Then I couldn't keep it to myself anymore and had to tell you what was on my mind. I can't put into words the shock I felt when you said you felt the same. My heart started to hammer and skip beats. I found it hard to breathe, but the words still left my mouth; and I told you everything I was feeling. The attraction. The longing. The fears. Every emotion I kept inside I told you. Never have I believed in fate or destiny more than I do now because you found me. Every time I think of you, I can't help but smile. A warmth fills me just thinking about you and your beautiful brown eyes. How strong your arms are and how I long to feel them hold me every night. It's your chest I want to fall asleep on listening to your heart beating in a lullaby just for me. Counting the days until I am in your arms and being with you seeing that beautiful smile. You found me and forever will I be grateful.

Souls United

Feeling your arms around me as our bodies move together as one. Pleasure washes over us as we both reach our peak. Names moaned as our mouths connect. Sweat covering our skin while our hearts hammer in our chests. Looking in your eyes, I can't help but whisper I love you because you touch my soul in a way no one ever has before. Making love to you steals more of my heart every time our bodies touch. Just the soft caress of your hand over my skin sends chills through my body. Knowing you are the other half of me. The piece I have been looking for my entire life causes my heart to sing. You are the love of my life. The one true half that we dream about.

Lying in bed, we look out the window counting the stars as we steal kisses and caress each other's bodies. Feeling you slid inside me making me moan your name. My nails dig into your skin. Every time we make love, I know you are the one for me. Our bodies fit together like two missing puzzle pieces. Skin touching skin. Mouths connected as we drink in each other's souls. Your fingers held my body close to you as I moan your name each time you bury yourself deep inside me.

Looking in your brown eyes, I can't help but smile as your brush light kisses over my neck and shoulder. Your fingers tangle deep in my hair as you kiss me with a hunger only you possess. Rolling as the sheets tangle around us moaning your name, I hear you growl my name in my ear and can't stop the shiver that washes over me. You are my true love. And I am blessed to feel our souls unite.

Never Understood

All of my life, I have watched people fall in and out of love around me. Seeing the blissful looks on their faces as they hold each other close. Listening to the angry accusations when it's turned sour in the end. Wondering if this was what my life had in store for me. I drifted from shallow relationship to shallow relationship, never putting my heart into it because to me, I love you is eight letters just like bullshit. I saw what relationships had in store for you if you gave your heart to someone. Then I met him, and I let myself fall. I gave a piece of myself I never thought I would, and for a time, we were just as blissful as everyone I had seen in the past. But soon, tragedy struck, and his true colors were shown. There were no angry words. No shouting or even words spoken in anger. Just locked myself away in a box safe from ever hearing those false words again. I held my pain inside for so long, it was as if it were eating me alive. I didn't care that he left. I didn't care that he lied. I couldn't overcome the lose that I suffered and struggled to deal with alone. Never getting to hold her or count her fingers or her toes. Never getting to see her smile or hear her giggle. And he walked away showing it didn't matter. I made a promise to myself never again would I fall for those words. Never again would I say those words. And for so long, I held firm to that promise. Until you said hello. It started as just talking and laughing. You made me smile when my skies were grey. Within days, I knew I was in trouble because my mind couldn't think of anything but you. Seeing your smile in my dreams. Aching to be held in your strong arms. Knowing you had been through pain too. Both a little cautious yet we fell anyway. Never have I been more grateful than I am right now that you said hello. You showed me what true love is. You showed me that love isn't just words. The way you treat me makes me melt, and the conversations we have that no one else would ever understand. You snuck into my life with a simple hello and stole my heart. I knew I loved you, and suddenly, all the love songs made sense to me. I lay awake at night thinking of you. Wishing I was curled up in your strong arms. Every time I hear the tone, I can't help but smile as I pick up the phone knowing it's you. I've tried and tried to think of the words to tell you how I feel. You are the missing piece of me. That piece you're told you only find once. I never understood what that meant until you. Now I don't think I could live without that piece because that would mean living without you. Not a breath leaves my body without you being the air I breathe. That last thing I'm thinking of when I close my eyes at night and the first thing I think of in the morning. I never understood what true love was until you said hello.

Hold on to You

Never thought it was possible to feel like this. A warmth is wrapped around me that I never dreamed would happen. Just lying in my bed reading our conversations over and over. Laughing at the funny parts and moaning at the sexy parts. The way you make me feel is so hard to put into words. So much joy fills me at the simple thought of us together. Knowing you are my forever. My one that I have looked for all my life. Your soul is my mate that all the books and movies talk about.

Fear of losing you has never been more real than it is when we're apart. Knowing how different our lives are. Thinking of all the things that could take you from me. My heart aches at the thought of not having you. Not holding you. Never reading new words from you. Tears burn my eyes as I lay in bed at night alone. All I want is to hold on to you.

You comfort me and tell me how much you love me. I feel the comfort in your words. Dreaming of your lips on mine and your arms around me. Feeling your fingers brush my skin. My heart is yours. Forever and ever. Until the end of time.

Friday Night

Lying in bed thinking of you. Feeling every nerve in my body come to life.

Lighting brushing my fingers over my wet folds imagining it was your fingers.

Moaning softly as I stroke a little bit harder dipping my fingers inside my core.

Your name is on my lips as my body arches picturing you pushing inside me.

Juices coat my fingers as they move faster and slid deeper. Calling your name

my body arches as I start to rub my nipples with my free hand. Hard pebbles aching

for your tongue to caress them. Opening my eyes, I see you watching me, and I rub harder

moaning louder letting you know how wet I am for you. Feeling a wave start to wash

over me when suddenly I feel your mouth on my nipple sucking and biting making me

cry out. Your fingers cover mine as your start to stroke my core coating your finger.

Your tongue circling my nipple, I whisper your name. You move my fingers and press your

hard warm shaft into my moist core. Crying out as your press deeper into me. I pull your

mouth to mine and kiss you with a hunger I didn't know I had. Our bodies move together

thrusting and pulling as we let the pleasure wash over us. Moaning for you to go deeper

inside me and begging you to go harder. We both started breathing heavy as our bodies

begin to quiver as my climax hits. My cum coats your shaft as I scream your name
feeling you swell inside me before your release hits and you cum deep inside me. I dig
my nails into your skin and hold you close as our bodies quake. You capture my mouth
in a passionate kiss. Our tongue dance while our arms wrap around each other and start to
move again. Our lust cannot be quenched. Thrusting harder and fast, I cry out against your mouth
and hold you tighter. Wrapping my legs around your waist, I meet your thrust with every rock of my
hips. Pulling my mouth away, I bury my face in your neck and whisper how much I love you as our bodies
meet in a frenzy of lust. Feeling my orgasm hit, I scream your name and arch against you, taking you deeper
inside my wet folds. You fill me once again with your seed moaning my name and holding me
tight giving one last thrust deep and hard inside me before you press your forehead against mine.
The words I love you don't feel strong enough. Our bodies still, and we catch our breath. Laying my
head against your chest, I listen to your heart pounding. I love you slips past my lips, and we lay in the tangled sheets.

Simply You

Everyone asks themselves what they want in this world, and sometimes the answers are easy. People want money. People want fame. People want honesty. Most of all, people want love. And I ask myself a hundred times a day what is it I want in this crazy mixed-up thing I call life. And I think of all the things I could possibly wish for. I could wish on every star every night to make me famous. But it's simply a wish for you. Simply you. That is all I could ever ask for in this world that would make me happy. The thought of seeing your warm eyes every morning when I wake up, and the thought of falling asleep in your strong arms against your chest feeling your heartbeat against me. That is what I truly wish for on all the shooting stars I see. It's you I wish for every second of every day. You fill my soul with longing to be with you. It's your hands I dream of caressing my body. Your lips I taste whenever a kiss plays in my mind. Your body I make love to in all of my dreams. Time and time again, I tell myself a wish is simply a wish. They don't come true. It's something our parents tell us when we are children to give us hope for the future. Something to think about and fantasize about. Then you said help, and your words caused my heart to hammer and my mind to wonder. Every time I make a wish, it's for one thing. And that one thing is simply you.

The Fall We Fear

Growing up, I was told many times about how painful love is. And promised myself it would never happen to me. I would never let anyone close enough to make me feel like that. And for so long, I never did. I imagined what it would be like to be like every other person in the world. That I didn't live to protect myself. But I also saw how much pain people around me went through when their love turned sour. And once again, I reminded myself I was living the way I should. People tell me I need to let go and find my one. But is there really just one? So many times, I hear them say they found the one over and over again. If there is only one, then how can you find it so many times. I never wanted to feel that way. Until I found you. Then it suddenly became the fall we fear. Only with you, there was no fear. I knew without a doubt you were and always will be the one. I didn't fear the fall. Because I knew you were there to catch me. And even if for someone reason you were to leave my life, I know I had no reason to fear the fall because I am better simply for knowing you. You bring me joy. You bring me fear. You bring me tears and laughter. But above all, you bring me love. And show me that there is no reason to fear the fall. Only to embrace it and enjoy every single second of it. You fill my heart with emotions I never dreamt I would feel. For that I thank you. For being my first and only.

About the Author

Laura is a single mother who is extremely devoted to her son. She is a huge lover of all kinds of books and different music. *Thoughts in a Journal* was the book she wrote to release her emotions.

CPSIA information can be obtained
at www.ICGtesting.com
Printed in the USA
LVHW030711160321
681657LV00010B/220